Beeston Cas

Robert Liddiard and Rachel Mc

Introduction

Standing on a rocky crag high above the Cheshire plain, Beeston is one of the most dramatically sited medieval castles in England. A fortification has existed on the cliff since early prehistoric times. The crag was an important centre for metalworking in the Bronze Age and a number of highly prized bronze objects have been found on the site. Occupation continued in the Iron Age, and the banks and ditches of a substantial Iron Age hillfort lie beneath the later medieval defences.

Ranulf, sixth earl of Chester (1170–1232), one of England's greatest medieval barons, began to build the castle at Beeston in the early 1220s. Parts of the surviving fabric date from this time. The castle soon passed to the Crown and a good deal was spent on it in the 1240s, but the domestic buildings were probably never fully completed. What we see at Beeston today is the defensive shell of a 13th-century castle that always retained a grim, austere quality. Despite several centuries of neglect, the castle was important enough in the 17th century to be refortified and was besieged for many months between 1644 and 1645 during the Civil War. After its surrender, the castle was partly demolished and the ruins became a popular destination. In the early 19th century the castle ruins provided a picturesque view from the vast new Peckforton Castle on the opposite hillside. Later Beeston became the site for the celebrated Bunbury Fair – a charitable fête attended by thousands of visitors in the later 19th century.

Above: An early 14th-century manuscript illustration of Henry III (1216–72). He took control of Beeston Castle in 1237, and extensive building works were carried out there during his reign

Facing page: A view from the top of Beeston Castle looking east. The crag is 155m high and, on a clear day, the view stretches as far as the Peak District, some 30 miles away

Tour

FOLLOWING THE TOUR

The tour begins outside the Victorian ticket office. Visitors should then climb the hill to explore the outer ward, or enclosure, of the castle and then the inner ward. The numbers beside the headings highlight key points on the tour and correspond with the small numbered plans in the margins.

Standing high on a prominent crag, which overlooks the flat landscape of Cheshire, Beeston Castle was built to impress. The castle consisted of an outer ward with an imposing gatehouse and curtain wall, and an inner ward, where the principal buildings were located. Today, the inner ward is the focus of the site. Built by Earl Ranulf of Chester in the 13th century, it has a deep, rock-cut ditch, a substantial gatehouse, one of the deepest wells in the country, and views that stretch for 30 miles in all directions.

OUTER WARD
▮ Ticket Office and ▯ Outer Gatehouse

The ticket office, which resembles the medieval gatehouse, and the stone wall that runs around the base of the crag, were built in 1846 by Lord Tollemache. Tollemache owned Beeston and the neighbouring estate of Peckforton at that time, and had his new residence of Peckforton Castle also designed in a medieval style. From the ticket office, the wide path leads up to the ruined outer gatehouse, the entrance to the medieval castle. Though the gatehouse has lost the upper storeys and battlements it once had, it still gives an impression of strength.

The inner and the outer gatehouses at Beeston were probably the first parts of the castle to be built by Earl Ranulf of Chester in the 1220s; the inner first and the outer second. As well as offering protection for the castle entrance, the gatehouse provided accommodation on the upper floors. Unlike many castles, no great tower, or keep, was ever intended at Beeston; rather, the emphasis was on the inner and outer gatehouses. Such a design is significant because, during the 1220s, the idea of enclosing the entrance to a castle within a gatehouse – rather than through a single tower or through the curtain wall – was a relatively new form of building in which royal castles such as Dover and Scarborough had taken a lead. The outer gatehouse at Beeston is one of the earliest examples of its kind built by a baron in England. It amply demonstrates Earl Ranulf's status as one of the leading magnates of the realm.

The outer gatehouse was essentially the same design as its counterpart in the inner ward. It was probably twice the

Below: The 19th-century ticket office has two towers and a gateway, and is a miniature version of the inner ward gatehouse. Victorian visitors paid to visit Beeston here. The buildings on either side of the towers were built in 1984 to house the exhibition and ticket office

Facing page: The outer curtain wall looking south towards the outer gatehouse

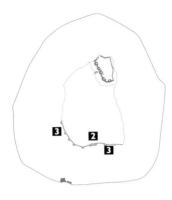

height of the remains we see today, as originally it would have been higher than the curtain walls. From outside, the most obvious features are the two rounded towers that originally framed the entrance passage. This passage could be closed by at least one set of gates; the hole for the wooden beam to secure what would have been the outer gate can still be seen in the north wall of the southern tower. The passage was further strengthened by at least one portcullis and the vertical groove for this is also still visible here. The location of the beam and the portcullis indicate that, originally, the gate opened outwards. The front of the northern tower is not original; the plan of the medieval arrangement was relaid in 1989 using original stones. In the rear of the north tower are the remains of a window and two stone corbels that originally supported a wooden first floor. In the rear wall of the south tower are the remains of a doorway with the slots for a door and part of a window.

The outer ward, or enclosure, was the focus of much of the fighting during the Civil War siege of 1644 to 1645 but during the parliamentary demolition of the castle that followed the royalist surrender, the outer gatehouse was left intact, possibly because the parliamentary overseer lodged in the building. Activity continued in the outer ward long after the rest of the castle had been abandoned; in 1703 one George Walley was renting a 'house and close by the castle gate'. The ruinous state of the gatehouse today is probably due to the extensive quarrying that took place on the crag from the 1720s onwards, when it was partially demolished in order to improve the access for carts.

Below: The ruins of the 13th-century outer gatehouse with its two round-fronted towers. The tall tower beyond was a later addition to the gatehouse structure. Beneath the medieval gatehouse, archaeologists have found the entrance to a prehistoric fortification. This suggests that the medieval builders took advantage of existing features in the landscape

❸ Outer Curtain Wall and Wall Towers

The outer ward was defended by a masonry curtain wall with eight projecting towers. These defences look far more formidable from outside the castle than from within. This is because of the sloping ground on which the castle is built. The towers look taller from outside because the ground in front of the wall slopes away naturally. The number and location of the arrowslits in the towers add to the castle's menacing appearance.

The condition of the towers varies considerably. Some are ruinous with only their plan remaining, whereas others are in a reasonable state of preservation. With the exception of the tall square tower next to the outer gatehouse, the towers projected in a 'D' shape from the curtain wall. All but one of the towers were open-backed. If any rear walls did exist, they would have been made of wood. Originally, they had at least one storey above the level of the curtain wall battlements.

The towers and the curtain wall are not of the same date. The first tower was probably that immediately to the north of the outer gatehouse. Its dimensions closely resemble those in the inner ward and it is the only tower on the curtain wall to have a rear stone wall. It seems likely that, alongside the outer gatehouse, it was part of Ranulf's original castle of the early 13th century. The remaining towers were probably built in the early 1240s when Beeston passed to the Crown. The towers were probably built first and linked by the wall only at a later date, possibly in the mid- to late 1240s.

The date and purpose of the dramatic square tower next to the gatehouse is uncertain. It must have been built after the gatehouse and the curtain wall since it abuts both. In comparison with the rest of the castle this tower is poorly

Above: This photograph of Beeston from the 1950s shows the outer ward and curtain wall before the site was covered with trees and bushes. The outer curtain wall enclosed an extensive area, where ancillary castle buildings such as kitchens and stables would have been located

Below: This cutaway reconstruction shows one of the D-shaped curtain wall towers with wooden floors and an open back

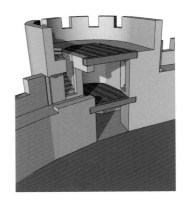

Ranulf III, sixth earl of Chester (1170–1232)

It is a measure of Ranulf's power that during his lifetime he was described as a 'prince'

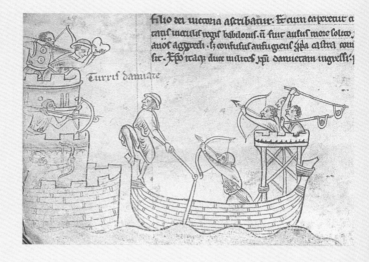

Turrif damiate

Ranulf III, the sixth earl of Chester and builder of Beeston Castle, was one of the greatest magnates of early 13th-century England. Ranulf was probably brought up in Cheshire; his nurse Wymarc was from a local family, and the county remained his power base throughout his career. He effectively made the earldom of Chester autonomous from royal government and it is a measure of his power that during his lifetime a monk at Chester described him as a 'prince'.

Ranulf's military exploits were impressive. He took part in several expeditions against the Welsh and played a leading role in the defeat of Prince Louis of France at the battle of Lincoln. In 1218 he joined the fifth crusade and a year later took part in the successful siege of Damietta in Egypt.

Following King John's loss of Normandy in 1204, Ranulf became a prominent figure in English politics, and was a chief supporter of King John and the young Henry III in their struggle against rebel barons. As a result of his loyal support he acquired extensive lands across England and showed remarkable political dexterity in maintaining his position during the period of royal recovery.

Ranulf died at Wallingford on 26 October 1232. His heart was buried at the Cistercian abbey he had founded at Dieulacres in Staffordshire, and his body was buried at St Werburgh's Benedictine Abbey in Chester. Despite two marriages, Ranulf had no children but he successfully secured adequate settlements for his co-heirs. His exploits soon passed into legend but perhaps the best image of Ranulf is that to be found on his seal, where he is depicted mounted and bearing arms, a reflection of both the chivalric ideal and the sometimes harsh political reality of his career.

built, with stones of various sizes haphazardly laid. It most likely dates from the late 14th or 15th century, a time when the castle was less important and high-quality work was not considered essential. The tower had a basement with two floors above. Latrines in these rooms emptied via two square openings that can just be seen above the earthwork bank on the south wall of the tower.

It is unclear whether the curtain wall originally formed a complete circuit enclosing the whole of the outer ward. A small piece of masonry, possibly from a tower, was excavated in the north-west corner of the outer ward. On the basis of the intervals between the existing towers, there might have been five more towers along the curtain wall.

Changes were later made to the curtain wall. On the third tower to the south of the outer gatehouse, for example, both arrowslits have been partly blocked, probably during the Civil War, in order to enhance their suitability for muskets. The walls have also been repaired in relatively recent times. A map from 1874 shows a clear gap in the wall between the fourth and fifth towers. This gap was filled not long afterwards, probably to improve the appearance of the defences when viewed from Peckforton Castle.

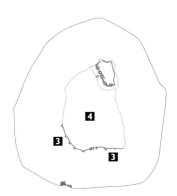

▣ Outer Ward Interior

The large area of the outer ward is today mostly covered by scrub and trees, but for much of Beeston's history this area was open ground. In prehistoric times it was occupied by at least nine huts known as roundhouses (see plan inside back cover), each of which would have accommodated a family. Loom weights for use in making textiles were found here, and indicate the kinds of domestic activities that took place.

During the Middle Ages the outer ward was presumably filled with ancillary buildings for the castle, although there is

Below: This view of the castle made by the Buck brothers in 1727 was perhaps taken from the hill on which Peckforton Castle stands. It shows the crag without the trees that cover the site today. In front of the inner ward, the artists have labelled 'a dry ditch'

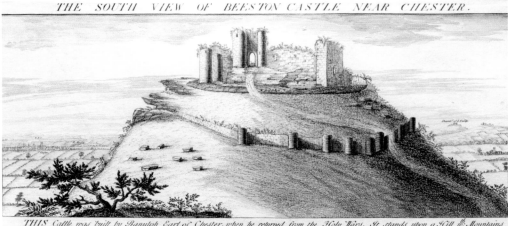

THE SOUTH VIEW OF BEESTON CASTLE NEAR CHESTER.

THIS Castle was built by Ranulph Earl of Chester, when he returned from the Holy Wars. It stands upon a Hill the Mountains on each Side, it takes up a vast extent of ground, and had strong Walls with many Towers, and was supplied with Water from a Well in the highest part of it, formerly of a great depth, but now almost filled up with Rubbish. An Antient Family of Beestons, (from w S* William Beeston late Governour of Jamaica descended) take their Name from this Town, & Castle ____ The present Owner is S* Ro: Weston Bar:*

S. B. delin: N. B. Sculp. 1727.

little archaeological or documentary evidence for such structures. There is a reference to a chapel in the 1240s, probably located somewhere in the outer ward, or possibly within the outer gatehouse.

In a hollow diagonally opposite the square tower, to the south of the outer gatehouse is one of the castle wells. It dates to the Middle Ages and was used throughout the castle's history. Although now almost entirely filled, in 1623 its depth was recorded as 240ft (73m). The crudely cut rectangular head of the well at the base of the hollow is probably the result of an attempt to enlarge it at some point, perhaps during the Civil War.

During the 18th century the chief activity on the northern side of the crag appears to have been quarrying. Sand was extracted and a stone quarry in the outer ward is also documented. A 'horse causeway' used to transport the stone is mentioned in 1722; this is probably the main path that visitors use today. In 1759 payments for gunpowder attest to the blasting of rock and there are blast marks on some of the quarry pits. The stone taken from the crag at this time was used to build cottages in the area and possibly for road building, while the sand was taken for industrial use, probably to the shipyards on the north Wales coast, owned by the Mostyn family, who held the Beeston estate at that time.

Towards the northern side of the outer ward a number of flat terraces may represent a levelled area associated with the encampment of troops during the Civil War or, more likely, the areas occupied by the tents and stalls of the 19th-century fairs held at Beeston Castle.

INNER WARD
5 Inner Ditch and Ramp

At the end of the path leading up the crag, a great rock-cut ditch separates the outer ward from the inner ward. The inner ward was the heart of the medieval castle; it contained the most important residential accommodation and was where, as a last resort, the garrison could hold out against attackers.

The rock-cut ditch is entirely man-made and dates to the earliest phase of construction in the 1220s. The stone quarried from the ditch was used for the castle buildings. The modern bridge was built in the 1970s, but remains of the medieval access to the inner ward can be seen below it.

In the 13th century, the ditch was crossed by a bridge, probably made of wood and supported in part by a pillar of rock left in place when the rest of the ditch was quarried. From 1303 to 1304 documentary sources tell us that a major redevelopment of the entrance took place and that a causeway and a new bridge were built. The large jumble of masonry that can be seen beneath the present bridge is all that is left of this causeway. It encloses the original 13th-century stone pillar, which can just be seen beneath the modern bridge. The causeway did not completely span the gap across the ditch and there must have been some kind of drawbridge allowing access to the inner ward. Evidently it was still thought necessary at this time to allow any defenders in the inner ward to completely shut themselves off from the rest of the castle in the event of a siege.

DITCH AND GATEHOUSE

1 Rock-cut ditch

2 Masonry from 14th-century causeway

3 South-west tower

4 Modern bridge (built 1975)

5 Inner gatehouse

6 Inner ward curtain wall

A RECONSTRUCTION OF BUILDING WORK AT THE CASTLE IN 1303–4

Conjectural buildings

A A timber-framed kitchen might have stood in the inner ward

B A temporary mason's workshop might have been built in the inner ward

1 Inner gatehouse

2 South-east tower

3 South-west tower

4 Inner ward

5 Inner ward well – it might not have been in use at this time

6 Ditch

7 Outer ward

8 Location of outer ward well

6 Inner Gatehouse

The inner gatehouse is a better surviving version of the one in the outer ward. The similarity between the two is clear and it is likely that the inner gatehouse was the first structure of the castle to be built as part of Ranulf's design in the early 1220s. Two towers enclose the entrance passage, which was defended by two arrowslits on either tower. There were two sets of gates; the sockets for the hinges can be seen on either side of the passage as can the holes for a wooden drawbar and the vertical grooves for the portcullis, which was drawn up through a slot overhead into the room above the gateway. The gatehouse had two ground-floor chambers on either side of the entrance passage, with a single room at first-floor level extending across the length of the building. The supports for the wooden floor can be seen in both sets of towers. Access to the first floor was at the rear of the gatehouse, probably by an external wooden stair.

The inner ward gatehouse was the most important building at Beeston Castle. The constable, who ran the castle on behalf of the lord or king, probably lived here and, as a high-status part of the castle, it was one of the areas most likely to be updated over time. The principal accommodation was to be found in the upper floor. A window was inserted in the rear of the gatehouse in the 14th century, probably to improve the accommodation.

7 Inner Ward Towers and Curtain Wall

Access to the towers and curtain wall was from the upper floor of the gatehouse and a blocked door at first-floor level can be seen within the western gatehouse tower. Excavations have shown that there was a fireplace on the first floor of the south-west tower. This is the only place in the castle where a fireplace has been found. Perhaps this heated room was a private chamber for the constable, with the gatehouse itself

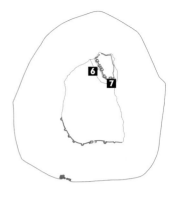

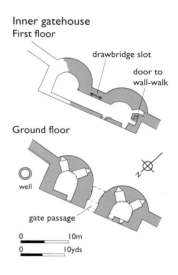

Inner gatehouse
First floor

drawbridge slot
door to wall-walk

Ground floor

well

gate passage

0   10m
0   10yds

Left: The inner ward from the air. This was the heart of the castle. The uneven surface of the interior suggests that there were never many permanent buildings here. For a key to the inner ward, see the drawing on the facing page

Peckforton Castle

Peckforton was so
convincing that it was
remarked at the time
that it would have
withstood an attack by
a medieval army

*Above: A sketch from 1851 of
Peckforton Castle by its architect
Anthony Salvin. The ruins of Beeston
Castle, which are shown in the
distance, influenced his design*
*Below: A portrait of John Tollemache
made in the 1840s*

John Tollemache was a major landowner in 19th-century
Cheshire and eventually held almost 26,000 acres in the county.
He took a close interest in the management of his estate and
spent a considerable amount of money on maintaining farm
buildings, land drainage and timber plantations. 'The only real
and lasting pleasure derived from the possession of a landed
estate' he wrote, 'is to witness the improvement in the social
condition of those residing on it.' His activities as a landowner
were in part politically motivated; he was a staunch Tory and
supporter of the landed interest and served as a Member of
Parliament for south Cheshire from 1841 to 1868 and for west
Cheshire from 1868 to 1872.

In 1840 he bought the Peckforton estate, which encompassed
Beeston Castle and the opposite hillside. As it had no existing
residence, between 1844 and 1852 he commissioned the
architect Anthony Salvin to build Peckforton Castle, at a cost
of £52,000. While it was not unusual for an aristocrat to spend
this amount of money on a country seat, this remarkable
building represented an attempt to recreate a medieval
fortress. Peckforton was so convincing that it was remarked at
the time that it would have withstood an attack by a medieval
army. The choice of site on the hill directly opposite Beeston
and the works on the medieval ruins undertaken at the same
time also suggest that, while undoubtedly the design of an
eccentric, Peckforton was intended to complement and
enhance the picturesque beauty of the landscape. Tollemache
died at Peckforton after being taken ill following a tour of his
Cheshire estate in 1890 and since the Second World War the
family have lived at their seat at Helmingham in Suffolk.

and other towers heated by braziers. The south-east tower contains the remains of a latrine on the first floor, which could also be reached from the curtain wall off the gatehouse.

The only part that gives some indication of the original appearance of the curtain wall is to the east of the inner gatehouse, where five battlements survive. Beneath the parapet are six square holes for the wooden beams of a hording – a gallery that protruded from the wall and allowed missiles to be dropped onto attackers in the ditch below. Below the battlements at the foot of the eastern wall is a blocked opening, capped with a lintel. This was probably a gun port cut through the curtain wall during the Civil War.

Despite considerable archaeological investigation, practically no evidence has been found for any major buildings such as a great hall or kitchens in the inner ward. Although such buildings might have been planned, it would seem they were not built. It also appears to have been a long time before the inner ward was completed, if it was ever finished at all. The north curtain wall was probably built in the 1280s and as late as the 14th century the upper storeys of the gatehouse and towers were finished in wood. In addition, the interior of the inner ward is rocky and uneven, and no attempt has been made to level the ground surface. Its condition seriously detracts from the visual approach into the inner ward, something that medieval lords normally wished to make imposing. All of this suggests that the castle was never finished. The ruined state of the inner ward is mostly the result of destruction after the Civil War.

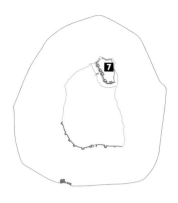

Below: The curtain wall survives to its full height in the south-east corner of the inner ward. The battlements, and the sockets for beams that supported a defensive wooden gallery, called a hording, are best seen from the outer ward

Above: Quarrying for sandstone in the outer ward of the castle during the 18th and 19th centuries created a network of caves that extend 20m into the natural rock

8 Inner Ward Well

The first documentary reference to wells at Beeston is in the 1230s, indicating that the inner ward well is contemporary with the early phase of the castle's history. In 1304, during major building works, payments are recorded to women for carrying water to the building site in the inner ward from a distance of one furlong; the approximate distance to the well in the outer ward. This suggests that the well in the inner ward was not in use for some reason at that time.

The exact depth of the well has long intrigued visitors to Beeston. In 1794 it was reported that it was filled to within 90yds (82m) of the top, but was 160yds (146m) deep. A long-standing tradition that King Richard II left treasure for safekeeping at Beeston in 1399 (see page 26) has led to several attempts at exploration. The most determined effort took place in 1842 when it was cleared out to a depth of 111m and the current protective coping constructed. The well has been explored twice in recent times: from 1935 to 1936 and in 1976. On the first occasion the depth was

Below: A view south-west from Beeston's inner ward looking out over the sheer cliff edge known as Pulpit Rock. Beeston Castle can be seen for many miles, and it is likely that Ranulf chose the site deliberately to make a bold show of his power and importance

The Surrounding Landscape

The view from the inner ward is one of the most dramatic in Cheshire. On a clear day the following places can be seen: to the west, the Welsh Hills (30 miles); to the north-west,

recorded at 110yds (100m), with medieval masonry to a depth of 200ft (61m). Thereafter the shaft was cut through sandstone. This would make the well one of the deepest at any castle in England. Intriguingly, three openings off the well shaft were located: one is a tunnel 9m long but, as it does not appear to lead anywhere, its purpose is unclear. Whatever the explanation, it is certain that, if it was ever deposited here, King Richard's treasure has long since disappeared.

9 CAVES

The south-east part of the outer ward preserves some remarkable caves. In the 19th century they were known as 'Beresford's Caves', supposedly named after a local inhabitant who made a living from quarrying sandstone. The stone was so soft that it could be easily crushed and the resulting sand was used in an early form of industrial sandblasting for cleaning the hulls of canal boats. Access to the caves is currently prohibited for safety reasons, and they are now home to a colony of bats.

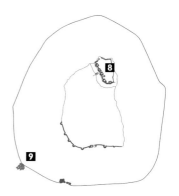

Chester (10 miles) and Ellesmere Port and the Stanlow oil refinery (13 miles); to the north, Liverpool (22 miles) and the Shropshire Union Canal (1 mile); to the east, Jodrell Bank observatory (18 miles) and the Pennines (30 miles); to the south, the Wrekin (30 miles); to the south-west on the opposite hillside, Peckforton Castle (1 mile). The slight sinuous ridges in the pastures to the north of the castle are the remains of former strips in medieval open fields, known as 'ridge and furrow'.

1 Peckforton Castle
2 Pulpit Rock
3 Mid-Cheshire Ridge
4 Welsh border
5 Former medieval open fields
6 Welsh Hills

History

Beeston Castle stands on a crag which has been occupied from prehistoric times, although the castle itself was not built until the 13th century. Following turbulent times in the Middle Ages and again during the Civil War, when the castle played a key strategic role, Beeston Castle found a new role in the 19th and 20th centuries as the picturesque backdrop to nearby Peckforton Castle and as the location for a succession of charitable fêtes.

PREHISTORIC BEESTON

The history of human activity on the crag long predates the building of the castle. Beeston was also important in the prehistoric period. Beneath the medieval gatehouse and curtain wall are a series of prehistoric defences dating to the later Bronze Age and the Iron Age (from c.900 BC to AD 40). The availability of metal deposits on the crag, together with the dramatic setting, marked Beeston out as a place of particular significance in the prehistoric landscape and flint tools dating to the Neolithic period (c.3,500–2,000 BC) have been found on the hill. It is possible that Beeston's crag was of ritual significance. This suggestion is strengthened by the likelihood that there were early Bronze Age burial mounds, now long since vanished and only known from fragments of pottery associated with burials, recovered during excavations on the lower part of the slope.

THE BRONZE AND IRON AGES

During the Bronze Age, Beeston's prominence in the landscape was marked by the building of an earthwork bank where the medieval outer curtain wall now stands. The bank cut the crag off from the surrounding countryside. It is unlikely that the early bank was a serious fortification; rather, it probably signified the importance of the activities that took place within the enclosure. Moulds and crucibles for smelting were found on the site, and indicate that at this time Beeston was a major centre for metalworking. The most remarkable finds were two copper-alloy socketed axes that had, apparently, been deliberately buried beneath the earthwork bank. These highly prized objects were perhaps left here for ritual purposes, giving some indication of the importance of the crag to the Bronze Age smiths who worked on the site.

The status of Beeston as a special place within the landscape continued into the Iron Age when, by stages, the Bronze Age enclosure developed into a hillfort. Hillforts were large enclosures, usually with substantial earth and timber defences. In southern England their development has been linked to the growth of powerful tribal units, where they

Above: A Stone Age arrowhead (top) and scraper (below), excavated in the outer ward at Beeston. Flint and stone tools and fragments of Neolithic pottery represent the earliest evidence of human activity on the site

Left: These bronze axe heads were discovered at Beeston. The axe in the middle was one of two that seem to have been placed beneath the Bronze Age rampart deliberately

Facing page: This 18th-century engraving is supposedly based on an early 17th-century drawing of the castle, which is now lost. Many of the details look fanciful, but the original drawing would have been the earliest view of the castle

Bronze Age Discoveries

The Bronze Age artefacts excavated at the castle constitute one of the most important collections of its kind in England

The Bronze Age (c.2,000–650 BC) was a period of considerable development in metalworking and by the late Bronze Age casting techniques were relatively sophisticated. The bronze artefacts excavated at the castle constitute one of the most important collections of its kind in England.

The implements found include five socketed axes with decorative ribs, one socketed axe decorated with flat facets, and a socketed knife. Socketed tools had a hollow recess where they could be fitted onto the end of a wooden shaft or handle, and secured in place. Other bronze items included a spearhead with a leaf-shaped blade and a peg hole to secure the shaft to it, and fragments of two sword blades – the only definite examples found in Cheshire. The objects fit into what is known as the 'Ewart Park' phase of bronze production, named after an important hoard of metal objects found at Ewart Park in Northumberland, which contained similar bronze implements to those found at Beeston. The Beeston artefacts date from between the ninth and eighth centuries BC, just before the advent of ironworking. Crucially, the remains of clay moulds and crucibles were also recovered, suggesting that metalworking was carried out on the crag itself. Copper ores could be found at the foot of Beeston's crag, as well as in the Peckforton hills, and the Bronze Age metalworkers at Beeston might have made use of these.

The majority of the artefacts recovered at Beeston were found in the outer ward, and probably represent the debris of metalworking discarded by the prehistoric smiths. Certainly not scrap metal, however, were two axe heads deposited beneath the bank of the prehistoric defences. Why these objects were so carefully placed here is not known, but they were possibly ritual offerings intended to mark the special significance of the metalworking site.

Below: These drawings show how wooden handles might have been fixed to Bronze Age blades found at Beeston to create an axe (left) and a knife (right)

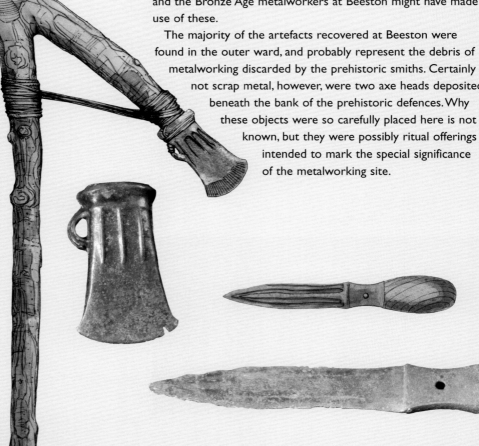

served not only as refuges but also as important places where agricultural surpluses, especially grain, could be stored in relative safety. Beeston might have served a similar purpose.

At Beeston during the early Iron Age (c.650–450 BC), the existing bank was made bigger and, for the first time, an accompanying external ditch was dug. The entrance to the fort was located on the site of the outer gatehouse and during archaeological excavation a cache of slingshot was recovered, perhaps suggesting a guard chamber there. The hillfort defences were again expanded in the late Iron Age (c.450 BC to AD 40) when a huge earthwork bank internally strengthened with stone rubble and topped with a wooden palisade was built along the line of the existing defences.

At the same time as the defences were being dramatically expanded, greater provision was being made on the site for storing and processing crops, especially cereals. Quantities of pottery that were probably used for the transportation of salt were also found. Cheshire was a major salt-producing area in the prehistoric period, and the storage of this valuable commodity at Beeston suggests that it was part of a wider regional trading network. Beeston was probably a focal point in the prehistoric landscape – a defended place protecting agricultural surplus and a centre for long-distance trade. It is not clear whether the hillfort extended over all of the area later occupied by the medieval castle, but this seems likely. If this were the case, then Beeston would have been the largest hillfort constructed in what later became Cheshire.

Despite its undoubted prehistoric importance, the hillfort was abandoned after the Iron Age. Roman pottery discovered at the base of the crag suggests that there was some kind of settlement in the vicinity, but other evidence for Roman occupation is not forthcoming. During the early Middle Ages woodland probably covered the area later occupied by the castle. The prehistoric entrance, however, must have remained prominent enough in the 13th century to be chosen as the site for the outer ward gatehouse.

Above: A Romano-British enamelled brooch, dating from the second century AD, found during excavations in the outer ward at Beeston Castle
Left: The Iron Age hillfort at Old Oswestry, about 20 miles from Beeston Castle. Beeston once had similar defences, although probably not on the same scale

Right: A 14th-century manuscript illustration showing masons at work on a castle. Like Beeston it sits on a hill and its towers and gatehouse are enclosed by a rock-cut ditch. In the foreground a king watches a mason draw out a design with a pair of callipers

EARL RANULF AND THE BUILDING OF THE CASTLE

Ranulf, sixth earl of Chester, began construction of Beeston Castle, or, to give it its medieval name, 'the castle of the rock', soon after 1220. One of the persistent myths concerning Beeston is that the castle was built in order to guard the vulnerable English border from Welsh raids. This argument does not stand up to scrutiny. During the final years of King John's reign (1199–1216), England was in the grip of a civil war between the supporters of the king and a baronial faction supporting the French king Philip Augustus and his son Prince Louis. Ranulf was a staunch supporter of King John and received titles, custody of castles and large parcels of land across England in return for his loyalty. When John died in 1216 his infant son, Henry III (1216–72), succeeded to the throne and during the first year of the new reign the French forces were defeated at the battle of Lincoln and the disaffected English barons were reconciled to the new king. As a reward for his services Ranulf received the earldom of Lincoln and he was a chief figure in arranging the peace agreement that led to the defeated French leaving England. In 1218, however, Ranulf left England to join the fifth crusade, fulfilling a vow he had made to King John three years before. Before he did so, he entered into a truce with his powerful neighbour, the Welsh prince Llywelyn the Great, prince of Gwynedd (c.1173–1240), whose lands lay to the west of Ranulf's Cheshire powerbase.

This alliance continued on Ranulf's return in 1220 and two years later Llywelyn's daughter Helen married Ranulf's nephew and heir, John le Scot. At the time the castle was built, therefore, the northern part of the English border was secure owing to Ranulf's alliance with Llywelyn the Great. Moreover, the castle stands to the east of Chester, rather than to the more vulnerable west of the county. The threat to Ranulf's position in Chester that led him to construct Beeston Castle came not from marauding Welshmen, but from power struggles within the English court.

As Henry III was a minor and could not rule in his own right, royal power was vested in the king's advisers. During the civil war of John's reign, men such as Ranulf, who had stayed loyal to the Crown, had received land, goods and offices in order to support their own positions and the royal cause. In the peace after 1217, however, their gains became a threat to royal authority and were a target for the king's justiciar, or viceroy, Hubert de Burgh (c.1170–1243). From 1220 Hubert moved guardedly, but decisively, against his opponents and over the next three years royal lands and offices were recovered and several high-profile barons were removed from their castles.

Although the precise date of construction is not known, shortly after returning from the crusade in 1220, Ranulf began to build his castle at Beeston and another at Chartley in Staffordshire, possibly from the proceeds of a tax throughout his lands. He probably also began to build Bolingbroke Castle in Lincolnshire at this time. The impressive gatehouses in the inner and outer ward and the tower to the east of the outer gatehouse at Beeston probably date from this time. The effort expended on these and the rock-cut ditch are witness to Ranulf's desire to show his potential strength. Beeston Castle was therefore a dramatic display of authority in Ranulf's principal earldom of Cheshire and a political gesture probably intended to resonate in England, not in Wales.

Ranulf did succeed in securing the majority of his lands and possessions, and ensured that his inheritance passed to his co-heirs, an event for which he had probably long planned. After his death in 1232, Beeston and the earldom of Chester were granted to Ranulf's nephew, John le Scot. On le Scot's death in 1237, Henry III seized the earl's lands and appointed John de Lacy, earl of Lincoln (c.1192–1240) as custodian of the county, including Beeston and Chester Castles.

It is not known how much of the castle had been built before the death of Ranulf. There are no documentary records of building expenses before the Crown took possession after the death of John le Scot and the amount expended afterwards suggests that, before the 1240s, much of the castle was incomplete. Some parts of the castle were inhabitable, and documentary references provide an indication of the nature of the castle buildings. In the late 1230s there were payments for the repairing of walls and also instructions to repair the castle well, including funds for a bucket, cable and a good rope.

Above: *Bolingbroke Castle in Lincolnshire was one of the three castles built by Ranulf*

Below: *This 13th-century manuscript illustration shows Hubert de Burgh as a penitent with bare feet and a cross kneeling at the foot of an altar. Ranulf built Beeston as a response to Hubert's growing power in the 1220s*

Above: A 14th-century manuscript illustration showing a hunting party with hawks in a wooded landscape. Hunting was a jealously guarded privilege of the nobility and Beeston would have been the setting for such activity throughout the Middle Ages

THE CASTLE UNDER ROYAL OWNERSHIP

Beeston was never a particularly important royal castle and was always subordinate to the castle at Chester. One early reference to Beeston in 1238 reports that the king demanded the use of eyries, or eagles' nests, at the castle. This was probably a requisition for birds of prey kept at the castle and might indicate that the area around Beeston was favoured for its hunting; certainly in the 14th century there was a park for hunting at neighbouring Peckforton. Beeston was maintained as the residence of a lord intermittently; between August 1237 and August 1238 payments are recorded for two knights and 30 sergeants to guard the castle. Beeston does appear to have had a role as a secure place within which to house prisoners: in 1245 orders were given that the king's hostages at Chester were to be transferred to Beeston.

A major programme of building works was undertaken in the 1240s, connected with the royal campaign against the Welsh in 1245. Understanding what exactly was built at this time is not easy, as payments for Beeston are frequently recorded together with those for other castles. Between

Christmas 1241 and Christmas 1242 a total of £410 12d was spent on repairing and fortifying Beeston and Rhuddlan. These were substantial sums and a clear indication that major works were ongoing at Beeston at this time. In 1245 another large sum was spent on finishing two turrets at Beeston, which may refer to the completion of the defences in the outer ward.

In 1253 or 1254 Henry III granted Beeston and the earldom of Chester to his son, the future King Edward I (1272–1307). The royal grant extended to the earl's heirs and so, from this date, Cheshire became part of the royal demesne, those lands that the Crown retained for itself. Edward came to Beeston in 1264 with prisoners taken after the battle of Evesham and stayed at the castle before forcing the surrender of Chester. During the campaigns into north Wales led by Edward, Chester was the principal military base for English expeditions.

BUILDING WORKS IN THE 14TH CENTURY
The early 14th century saw another major programme of rebuilding. Between September 1303 and September 1304 a considerable sum was spent on construction, indicating work far in excess of routine maintenance. The chamberlain William of Melton and his successors recorded details of the expenditure and the accounts provide a detailed and vivid picture of the organization and an account of the operations.

The principal work took place in the inner ward where three towers were raised and crenellated 'because they formerly had high wooden surfaces, and now they are made level' – a valuable detail indicating that, despite the 13th-century works, the defences were not completely finished in stone. Presumably, before the new works, the towers were provided with wooden pitched roofs that had to be dismantled in order to allow the raising to take place. In addition a new bridge was constructed and a 'great massive stone wall before the said bridge' 34ft high, 7ft thick and 20ft long, was built as a supporting structure. The remains of it can be seen today below the modern bridge.

Timber was brought by ox cart from Delamere Forest eight miles to the north-east, as well as spare lead trimmings from the roof of the great tower at Flint and lead from Northop near Mold. The lead was made into sheets by a monk called Thomas the Plumber who spent about 145 days fixing them on the roofs of the three towers. Further works took place in subsequent years. In 1305 under the direction of one Master Robert of Glasson, the outer gate in the outer ward was repaired and from 1312 to 1313 houses and towers at Beeston were mended and repaired by Robert the Carpenter of Kingsley and William the Plumber.

Below: A manuscript illustration of King Edward I (1277–1307). Edward's conquest of Wales at the end of the 13th century made Beeston finally redundant

When Edward III's eldest son was created earl of Chester in 1333 it was, perhaps unsurprisingly, reported in a survey that the castle was 'well and surely sited on a rocky eminence, and very well enclosed' and that no repairs were deemed necessary. This said, between 1359 and 1360 the castle was developed with timber taken from the park at neighbouring Peckforton. There are references to more works in the following years, most notably 272 days spent roofing the tower of the castle with lead.

King Richard II (1377–99) made Cheshire a principality in 1398 and in 1399 the king visited Chester before sailing on a military expedition to Ireland. On his return, he was captured by rebels led by Henry Bolingbroke, the future King Henry IV (1399–1413), and it is Richard's actions before his departure for Ireland that have given Beeston its most persistent legend: that the king hid part of the royal treasure somewhere in Beeston Castle. There may be an element of truth to the story, although the historical reality has been embellished and distorted. The contemporary *Kirkstall Chronicle*, written by a monk of Kirkstall Abbey in Yorkshire, states that, in the aftermath of Richard's capture, 'vessels and many other goods [were] found in water cisterns' and that more was taken from 'other secret places'. The *Dieulacres Chronicle*, written by a monk of Dieulacres in neighbouring Staffordshire before 1413, also records that Henry seized treasure and other valuables that had been buried. Such stories probably underlie attempts to investigate the well in the inner ward in 1794 and 1842, but the historical sources seem to make it clear that, after Richard's capture, Henry Bolingbroke recovered any treasure that had been dispersed in royal castles.

Above: Builders completing a tower use a hoist to lift stones in this 14th-century manuscript illustration. Work was carried out on the towers at Beeston Castle on a number of occasions in the early 14th century

Below: This manuscript illustration depicts the capture of Richard II at Conway. There is a long-standing myth that before his capture, Richard hid treasure at Beeston, which has never been discovered

LATE MEDIEVAL BEESTON

After 1400 Beeston appears to have been neglected. In the 15th century, porters were still recorded at the castle but the antiquarian John Leland (c.1503–52), writing in about 1540 reported that the castle was ruinous. Enough remained for William Camden (1551–1623) to describe it as 'a place well guarded by walls of a great compass, by a great number of its towers, and by a mountain of very steep ascent', and a late 16th-century account describes the castle inner ward 'with a Goodly strong Gatehouse, and a strong Wall, with other Buildings; which when they flourished, were a convenient Habitation for any great Personage', an outer 'wall furnished with Turrets' and 'first a fair Gate'.

In 1602 the manor of Peckforton, which included Beeston Castle, was sold to the local gentleman Sir Hugh Beeston for £2,500. His will (1626) records that his two poor relations, George and Richard Beeston, requested that they be maintained with 'house room and easements and commodities', that they 'hold and occupy within the walls [of the castle]', or be rehoused elsewhere. Clearly some occupation of the outer ward continued at this time, but the impression given by historical documents is that, on the eve of the Civil War, the majority of the castle was in ruins.

Above: A map of Cheshire drawn by Christopher Saxton in 1583. Beeston Castle is shown on a hill in the centre. It must still have been prominent in the landscape, despite not being of great importance at that time

Right: John, first Lord Byron, by
William Dobson, about 1643. He
was a royalist field-marshal in
Cheshire and led the defeat of the
parliamentarians at the second
battle of Middlewich in 1643

BEESTON IN THE CIVIL WAR

Following the outbreak of civil war in 1642, Cheshire had
supporters for both king and parliament, but there were also
many who remained neutral and those who waited upon
events before committing their allegiance. In the face of
considerable reluctance by local gentry to provide resources
for the war, the royalists and parliamentarians agreed a peace
treaty at Bunbury, near Beeston, in December that year. This
proved no more than a cover as both sides attempted to
raise money and men not only from Cheshire but also from
outside the county as the conflict between king and
parliament began to escalate into a national civil war.

The royalists established a base of operations at Chester,
which became their main port for men and supplies from
north Wales and Ireland. In contrast, the parliamentarians
were slower to organize their war effort in the county and it
was only in January 1643 that, under the command of the
puritan Sir William Brereton (1604–61), they were able to
establish headquarters at Nantwich.

The custody of Beeston Castle, sited in the centre of
the county, was therefore of interest to both sides who, by
February 1643, were scrambling to extend their control of
the countryside. Brereton's chaplain Nathaniel Lancaster later
commented that Brereton 'prized it [Beeston] by the
situation'. On 20 February, Brereton installed a parliamentary

garrison of between 200 and 300 men in the castle together with 'much wealth and other goods of the gentry and other neighbours brought thither for safety'. The state of the castle's defences was obviously a source of concern, however, as Brereton 'caused the breeches to be made up with mud walls, the well of the outer ward to be cleansed, and a few rooms erected'. Following a parliamentary victory at the first battle of Middlewich on 13 March, the garrison was secure and their occupation focused on the defences of the outer ward.

In the event, these efforts were of little consequence as in November 1643 royalist reinforcements from Ireland led by John, first Lord Byron (1559–1652), landed at Chester and began offensive operations against parliamentary forces. By this stage Beeston's garrison had been reduced to about 60 men with several officers seconded to different posts. The commander, Captain Thomas Steele, was later criticized by Nathaniel Lancaster as being 'a rough hewn man; no soldier whose care was to see it [the castle] repaired, victualled and [to] live quietly there, than the safe custody of it', though for his part in the events that followed, Steele himself felt that as a punishment for his sins God had robbed him of his courage. In an act of bravado in the early hours of 13 December 1643 'a litle before Daye, and after the Moon was sett', the royalist Captain Thomas Sandford and eight men got into the castle and took control of the inner ward; they probably entered via the north side of the outer ward and then made their way to

Above: A portrait of William Brereton, made in 1647. In 1643 Brereton was appointed commander-in-chief of the parliamentarian forces in Cheshire

Below: A near-contemporary drawing of the first battle of Middlewich, showing artillery and the position of troops. The fighting took place in and around the streets of the town, and in the churchyard of St Michael and All Angels' church

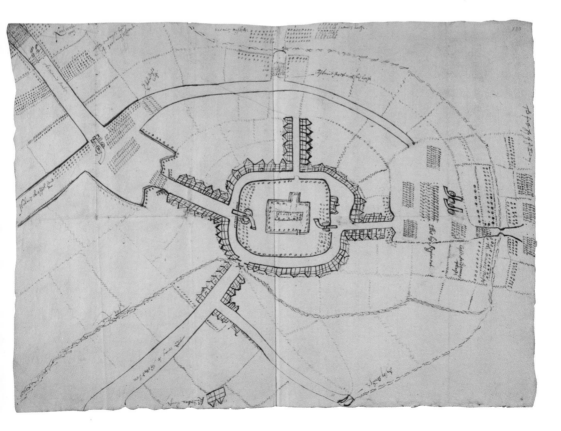

the top of the crag. Steele dined with Sandford in the outer ward, sent beer to Sandford's men, and agreed to surrender his 60 men. In reality Steele probably had little choice as the remainder of the royalist army was at the castle gates. He secured honourable terms for his men, who were allowed to 'depart with their colours and arms' the following day, but leaving the stored goods, material and equipment behind. The honourable terms of the surrender achieved by Steele were ultimately to no avail as he was tried and shot at Nantwich for his failure to offer a defence.

Byron garrisoned Beeston and shortly afterwards defeated the parliamentarians at the second battle of Middlewich on 26 December 1643. For nearly a year a royalist presence was maintained at the castle without incident, but in November 1644 Brereton besieged Chester and it became necessary to remove the threat of the royalist garrison at Beeston, which was more than capable of interfering with the siege. Brereton's men seized cattle from the area around the castle, successfully fought off a royalist attempt at recovery and billeted themselves in local farmhouses to maintain a blockade. The royalists resisted the efforts of the parliamentarians and on 7 December successfully raided a nearby house where 26 soldiers lodged, burning it to the ground and killing all but two of the occupants.

In order to make their blockade more effective, Brereton's men constructed fortifications in front of the outer ward. Brereton himself reported that 'we have almost finished a mount before Beeston Castle gate, which is encompassed with a strong, deep trench. This will command and keep them in the castle so that they dare not issue out in strong parties to annoy the country or bring in provision.' By May 1645 these fortifications were completed. During the summer the royalists destroyed them and the parliamentarians were forced to rebuild, this time erecting a fort within musket shot of the gate, which held 100 men and their supplies.

Above: This pewter dish, or porringer, was found during excavations of the inner ward at Beeston. It would have been used for eating soup or stew, and dates from the first half of the 17th century. It probably belonged to troops stationed at the castle during the Civil War

Right: A map showing Beeston Castle and the key locations in its Civil War history (1642–6)

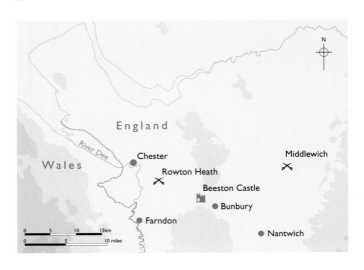

With the royalist garrison effectively hindering the wider parliamentary attempt to take Chester and establish control over the whole county, custody of Beeston became strategically more important in the latter stages of the war. The parliamentary attempt to take the castle and the equally determined efforts on the part of the royalists to raise the siege, nearly led to a major confrontation by field armies on at least one occasion in 1645 and, while a pitched battle never occurred, the royalists twice succeeded in relieving the castle, only for the parliamentarians to immediately resume their blockade.

It was wider political events that dictated the outcome of proceedings. With the defeat of the king at the battle of Rowton Heath two miles south-east of Chester on 24 September 1645 there was little point in further royalist resistance and the castle was surrendered on 15 November. The royalist commander, Captain Vallett, and his 56 men were allowed to leave with two carts and their colours flying. Twenty of his men immediately surrendered and were allowed to return to their homes, understandable when it is considered that conditions had become so bad that they had apparently eaten

Above: Part of a painted glass window in nearby Farndon parish church, which was commissioned in 1662 to commemorate the royalist forces who defended Chester. It shows military equipment as well as musketeers, pikemen, a standard bearer and musicians

Above: This halfpenny token of 1797 shows Beeston Castle on its crag. Coins such as these were minted by provincial manufacturers in the late 18th century to counteract the shortage of low-value coinage to pay workers in newly industrialized towns. Designs showing prominent local landmarks were often chosen
Below: By the 18th century, Beeston was valued as a scenic ruin. This view of the inner gatehouse by George Barret, of about 1760, shows the ditch already partly filled

their cats. Vallett's horse could barely carry him and the victorious parliamentarians found, 'Theire was neither meate, Ale nor Beere found in the Castle, save only a peece of Turkey pye, Twoe Bisketts, a lyve Peacock and a peahen.'

The day after the surrender Brereton ordered all munitions and stores to be removed from the castle and the destruction of the parliamentarian siegeworks. Chester itself surrendered on 3 February 1646 and the Civil War in Cheshire was over. In the aftermath, warrants were issued for Beeston and neighbouring castles to be slighted, that is demolished to be rendered indefensible. This order was carried out and it was reported that 'Onelie the Gatehowse in the lower warde and parte of some Towers in the higher warde, weire lefte standings, which scythens [since then] are pulled downs and utterlie defaced.' The graves of three young men were also excavated from the northern part of the inner ward; while undated, they most likely represent royalist casualties of the siege.

BEESTON AS A PICTURESQUE RUIN

After the Civil War the castle was again allowed to decay. A number of local folk tales circulated about the castle. Chief among these are the stories of the well in the inner ward and its treasure, but from the 16th century there were prophecies that the castle would one day rise to 'save' all England. King Edward VI was noted as the 'saviour' at least once, although to save England from what or from whom is not entirely clear.

During the 17th century the castle passed by marriage to the Denbighshire landowner Sir Thomas Mostyn (1651–c.1700) and, despite quarrying, the crag became something of a tourist attraction. The romantic situation of the ruins provided inspiration for numerous artists and for other items such as commemorative coinage; the Beeston halfpenny of 1797, shown opposite, shows the castle fancifully recreated.

In 1840 the aristocratic landowner John Tollemache (1805–90), later the first Lord Tollemache of Helmingham, bought the Peckforton estate, of which Beeston formed a part. Alongside the building of Peckforton Castle on the hillside opposite Beeston, he paid considerable attention to the ruins of its medieval counterpart. The works on Beeston Castle were extensive. Parts of the outer curtain wall were repaired, and because original stones were reused it is impossible to judge how much of the castle was rebuilt at this time. Certainly he had a great interest in the history of the

Above: John Tollemache, first Lord Helmingham, painted here a year before his death in 1890. He bought Beeston Castle and the neighbouring estate of Peckforton, where his new castle was built between 1844 and 1852. Peckforton is shown in the painting on the wall behind him

castle, and it was in this period that the well in the inner ward was first subject to systematic exploration. The clear attempt to alter the character of the site is also indicated by the planting of fir trees (then exotic imports) in the outer ward, probably to complement similar planting that surrounded Peckforton, and in 1868 fruit trees were planted near the castle gate. Deer were allowed to run over the outer ward, as were, somewhat curiously, kangaroos – another attempt to bring exotica into Tollemache's Cheshire estate.

The 19th century saw a dramatic increase in numbers of tourists visiting the crag. Access to the castle was greatly improved by the opening of the Chester to Crewe railway in 1846 and a station at Beeston. Then, as now, the well in the inner ward generated a great deal of attention and in the 1840s it was provided with a stone hut to stop visitors hurling objects down the shaft. The broad range of people who came to the castle and their activities are best illustrated by a late 19th-century guidebook which reported that Beeston was 'much visited by picnic parties through the summer months, from the tea party for the rustic school boy, with a slight and partial knowledge of the "three Rs: Reading, Riting, and Rithmetic", to the visits of the deep read antiquarian, archaeologist and geologist, who can find ample scope for their extensive powers of mind … On the grassy mountain sides, are to be seen the bounding roe, goat, Kangaroo and bleating sheep, and in great profusion the nibbling conies.'

In 1844 the first Beeston festival was held at the castle. It was organized by the branch of the Independent Order of Oddfellows from nearby Bunbury, a charitable organization

Above: An early photograph of the inner gatehouse at Beeston showing visitors to the castle and the overgrown condition of the inner ward. Before its restoration by the Ministry of Works in the 1960s, the ditch had been almost completely filled

Right: Beeston festival in 1851, as depicted in the Illustrated London News. *Peckforton Castle is shown on the left, and Beeston, with its tents, stalls and crowds of visitors, is on the right*

Left: Beeston Castle station for in a photograph from about 1905. Lord Tollemache apparently allowed the Chester to Crewe line to be built across his land on condition that express trains stopped at Beeston. The coming of the railways saw a dramatic upsurge in visitors to the castle, and in the late 19th century, extra services from Crewe and Chester were provided to bring visitors to the Beeston festival

that used the occasion to raise money for a Widows' and Orphans' Fund. The success of the festival — a clear profit of £94 was made — ensured that it became an annual two-day event attended by thousands of people. By the mid 1850s it had become known as the Bunbury Fair. The festival, together with the need to accommodate general tourists, led to the construction in 1846 of the gatehouse that now forms the ticket office. Access to the site was controlled by the construction of a stone wall running around the base of the crag, which also prevented the deer and kangaroos from escaping.

Beeston Castle was also used to celebrate major events: in 1897 Queen Victoria's Jubilee was celebrated with a bonfire and in 1902 a special fête marked the coronation of King

Above: Alec Irvine in a bosun's chair before he was lowered down to explore the well on 27 January 1935. The photograph appeared in Cheshire Life *magazine under the caption 'A thrilling moment'*
Below: A view from the upper ward, looking north across the Cheshire plain. Beeston remains popular both for its impressive ruins and for its spectacular setting

Edward VII. By 1906, the festival was making a loss because of the lack of a flat area on the crag for sports and the costs of transporting the necessary equipment. Thereafter the annual Bunbury church fêtes were held intermittently at the castle, but were a poor imitation of the Beeston festival. After 1945 the current Beeston Castle fête was established, which continues to be held every year on August bank holiday.

THE CASTLE AS AN ANCIENT MONUMENT

In 1959 the Ministry of Works took the site into guardianship, and in turn it passed to English Heritage in 1984. Much work was done to clear the site, particularly in the rock-cut ditch between the inner and outer wards, and parts of the castle were excavated to shed light on its development. Two series of excavations were carried out between 1968 and 1973 and 1975 and 1985, which transformed our understanding of the castle. In 1975, in order to make the site more accessible, the present concrete bridge leading to the inner ward was constructed. The chosen design and materials used ensure that this bridge is now of architectural interest in its own right. Today, Beeston is prized as a popular destination for walkers attracted by the castle's spectacular situation, one that has, in different ways, drawn people to the crag since prehistoric times.